DAVID COOK
LAND ANIMALS

CONTENTS

CROWN PUBLISHERS INC. NEW YORK

Animal conservation

Many wild animals in the world today are struggling for survival, and some are in serious danger of dying out altogether unless we take steps to protect them.

Life has never been easy for most wild animals. They have to look for food or hunt for it. They have to find and guard their own territory in which to breed and rear their young. And often there is the constant threat of being hunted and killed by the animals that prey on them.

Animals are used to coping with these difficulties, but now they are being increasingly exposed to new, and even greater hazards, as a result of our conquest of the world.

As the human population grows, we take over more and more land to meet our own needs. We build roads, railways, cities and factories. We convert the wild countryside into cultivated land to grow crops, build farms and rear livestock. When we take land for our own use, we destroy the natural habitat of wild animals, which are often left with nowhere else to go, and no alternative source of food. So their numbers diminish because there is not enough suitable land to support them all.

Humans have also endangered many species by excessive hunting. Animals are killed for food, for their skins, and for the many commercial products, such as cosmetics and medicines, which contain ingredients extracted from animals. Some animals are shot because they are regarded as pests which harm crops or kill livestock,

Polar bears live in the coastal areas of the Arctic Ocean. Hunting led to them becoming extremely rare in many areas.

But the nations which surround the Arctic Ocean made an agreement which gave the bears almost total protection.

and others are hunted for sport. All this takes a very heavy toll on the animals.

A hundred years ago, few people could foresee how seriously human activity in the world would affect the lives of wild animals. But now, almost too late, we have begun to realize that without help from us, many species (or kinds) of animals will perish, never to be seen again.

So the conservation movement has grown up. This is made up of different societies and organizations devoted to saving wild animals and their environment. They have a difficult task, and there is much work to be done. Research projects have to be set up in order to study the animals and find out how endangered they are, what their needs are, and what can be done to help them. Money has to be raised to buy land for nature reserves and sanctuaries where wild plants and animals can live undisturbed.

The animals are unable to speak for themselves, and the conservation movement provides a "voice" for them, urging world governments to protect and preserve them, and persuading people to stop hunting them and destroying their natural habitat. Already the movement has been successful in saving many species from extinction, and is fighting to save many more which are threatened.

It is not only the conservationists who care. More and more people are becoming concerned about the plight of wild animals. None of us would like to think of a future in which all our favorite wild animals had become extinct, and were only seen in books, films, or on the television screen. It would be sad to think of a world where the only surviving animals were family pets and farm livestock.

The numbers of koala bears in Australia fell to just a few thousand. They had been hunted for fur and had been further reduced by epidemics. Koalas eat only the leaves of some eucalyptus trees and many of these had been felled to clear land. But now they are no longer hunted and reserves have been established, planted with the trees they need to live.

5

Animals at risk

auroch
Europe 1627

warrah
Falkland Is. 1876

blaauwbok
South Africa 1799

quagga
South Africa 1883

white wolf
Newfoundland 1911

Schomburgk's deer
Thailand 1932

Bubal hartebeeste
North Africa 1923

Syrian onager
Middle East 1930

Extinct mammals
All these mammals
are extinct, destroyed
by people. The date
shown against each
animal is the year
when they probably
died out.

thylacine
Tasmania 1933

As living things evolve, they change in order to adapt to their surroundings. Some species are unable to adapt and become extinct. Others evolve into new kinds of species which are better equipped to cope with a constantly changing world. When a species becomes extinct naturally, or evolves into a new form, the process is very gradual and happens over a period of anything from thousands to millions of years.

Because humans have changed the world so rapidly in the last few hundred years, animals have not had time to adapt. This has meant that the evolution of new species is proceding too slowly to keep pace with the accelerated extinction of existing animals.

In the last four hundred years, 120 mammals have become extinct. Out of a total of 4,000 species of mammal, 120 may seem a fairly small number. But in fact this number gives very little indication of the true level of destruction that has taken place. It does not give any idea of the many animals which survive in such small numbers that they are in constant danger of dying out, or of the dwindling populations of many species which were once found abundantly.

The area that a species of animal inhabits is called a range. Although the range of many animals has remained the same, their numbers have fallen drastically.

Brown bears, or ursus arctus, are a good example of this. They have a huge range which extends right across the northern hemisphere of the world, in Europe, Asia and America. Cut off from each other by oceans, deserts and mountains, many subspecies (or races) of the bears have evolved, from the giant Kodiak grizzlies of Alaska, to the small brown bears from Syria.

European brown bears are now quite rare, and many subspecies are already extinct. The Mexican grizzly is the rarest of the world's large mammals, if it still survives.

However, because brown bears occupy such a large range over the world they are not in immediate danger of dying out altogether. As one race becomes extinct in one part of the world, the chances are that it will not die out elsewhere, where it might be protected. However, only a small number survive anywhere.

Bears have been ruthlessly hunted for meat and for their skins. Because bears are dangerous animals and sometimes prey on livestock, the men who hunted them were regarded as heroes. But now it is essential that they are saved from hunters in the remote areas where they still survive.

Brown rats were native to Asia but are now found across the world, carried as unwelcome passengers on ships.

Rats spread disease and damage property. But they are a good example of an animal which benefits from people.

The Mexican grizzly bear must be the rarest mammal in the world – if any now survive. Only 30 were found in all Mexico in 1960. Some people tried to save them, but cattle ranchers set out to destroy them. There is still some hope that a few survive, but it is probable that they are extinct.

7

Island-dwellers

Island-dwellers tend to be less adaptable than other animals because they have evolved in isolation.

In some cases the animals arrived on islands by chance, and in others they were cut off from the mainlands when the oceans rose. The problem for these species is that although they are well adapted to their natural surroundings, they are very vulnerable to changes brought in from the outside world. They are also very restricted, because if their island habitat becomes unsuitable for them, there is nowhere else for them to go.

The lemurs of the island of Madagascar illustrate this. These animals, related to apes, monkeys and humans, evolved in isolation. Since the arrival of people in Madagascar in the last two thousand years, several types have become extinct. The fifteen remaining species are now seriously at risk because more and more forest has been cleared for farming and settlement. Reserves have been declared for them, but only time will tell whether these strange-looking animals will survive.

Another very unusual island animal under threat is the giant tortoise, which has a life-span of over a hundred years. The ancestors of the giant tortoise drifted on to islands as far apart as those off East Africa and Ecuador. When sailors discovered the islands, the tortoises they found there were slaughtered mercilessly for their meat.

The remaining tortoises are now further threatened by animals which were intro-

Primates of Madagascar
All these odd-looking primates evolved in isolation on the island of Madagascar. Now most are threatened as the land there is cleared for farming.

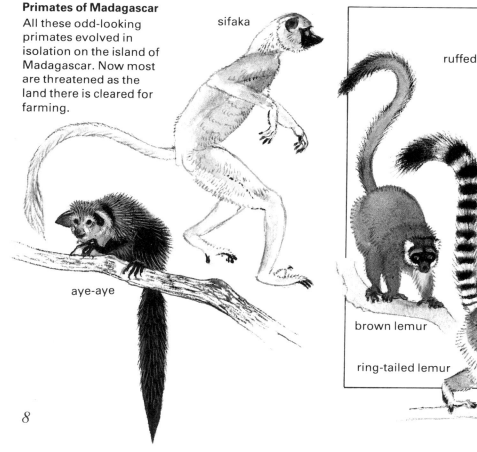

aye-aye

sifaka

ruffed lemur

dwarf lemur

brown lemur

ring-tailed lemur

duced on to the islands. Pigs and rats eat their eggs and their young, and goats destroy the vegetation on which they feed.

The Komodo dragon, which lives on the island of Komodo, in Indonesia, is an enormous lizard measuring more than six feet in length. The huge lizards have been in competition with local people because both hunt the wild pigs and deer. The Komodo dragons have become rare, as a result of being unable to find food.

The changes made on islands cannot be reversed. The conditions to which these unique animals adapted no longer exist. Only with the greatest care will they survive. But, if they are allowed to die out, then a little more of the variety of life in the world will have gone forever.

The giant Galapagos tortoise still lives in small numbers on the Galapagos Islands, where it is protected.

The rare Komodo dragons use their tongues to scent prey. They mostly eat carrion, like the young dead monkey shown here.

Mainland-dwellers

Gray wolves were once one of the most widely distributed mammals in the world (their range is colored green on the map).

Golden marmosets were commonly kept as pets, although few lived long away from their native forests in Brazil. As a result of the pet trade, and the destruction of the forests in which they live, they are now endangered.

Mainland animals, which live on the great land masses, are not as restricted as island-dwellers. They can retreat into the wilderness. But so much land has now been taken for human use that, in many cases, they are now confined to the remaining areas of natural habitat left unspoiled by humans.

Some, like wolves, are distributed all over the world in the remote regions left to them. But whereas there used to be vast numbers of them, wolves are now common only in Alaska and Canada.

Nearly half the world's animal species are to be found in the tropical rain forests. But these forests are fast disappearing as the trees are felled for timber, and the land cleared for crops. As a result, many animals are being deprived of their homelands. The woolly monkey and the marmoset, both familiar sights at a zoo, are now becoming extremely rare in the wild. Reserves have been set up for them, but because they live in trees they are difficult to study, and nobody knows how much land is needed to support them. Once the tropical forest has been cleared the land is only fertile for a few brief seasons. Then it becomes semi-desert, useless for farming, and ruined for the wild animals which once lived there.

Animals that live on a very specialized diet are particularly vulnerable to change. The panda, for instance, will eat practically nothing but bamboo shoots. Bamboo plants live for about a hundred years, then flower and die. Previously, when the plants died the pandas could simply move on to the next patch of luxuriant bamboo forest. But in western China, the home of the panda, much of the forest has been cleared, and there is now no bamboo left.

The situation is critical for the pandas

because the existing bamboo in one of their reserves in western China has already flowered and died. Very little bamboo is left in adjoining regions because the land has been taken for farming.

The fate of the panda is in the hands of the Chinese government and the World Wildlife Fund, who have jointly set up a "Save the Panda" campaign.

Giant pandas are only found in a few remote areas of China. The bamboo which they normally eat has died in some forests, so the "Save the Panda" campaign is looking for other food pandas will accept.

Hunting for profit

The meat and skins of wild animals are no longer needed to provide most people with food and clothing. Yet hunting still continues, and can be very profitable for hunters and others in the commercial world. The more animals a hunter kills, the more money he makes. And, the rarer an animal becomes, the higher the price it fetches. This makes hunters seek out the most threatened species, and so endanger them even further.

During the last century the beaver and the ibex were hunted to near extinction in Europe. Both were valued as a source of medical ingredients. In the case of the beaver, the prized ingredient was castor, a substance secreted by one of the animal's glands. Almost every part of the body of the ibex has been used in medicine, including its blood, which was thought to cure pneumonia. Extracts from these animals are no longer used for medicine, and the

Australian aborigines hunt animals, like the young kangaroo, for food. But there are few of them, and they have primitive weapons, so they do not harm the species. But now hunters armed with modern weapons are slaughtering the kangaroos for the petfood trade.

beaver and ibex have now been re-introduced to areas in which they were extinct until recently.

The rhinoceros has not been so lucky. The Asian and African rhinos have both suffered severe setbacks since the beginning of the century, and they are now very rare animals. This has happened because the land on which they used to live has been taken over for cultivation, and also because they have been continually hunted. In India, for instance, they were hunted for sport by the British who once colonized the country.

The most ruthless and widespread slaughter of the rhinoceros has occurred because the animal's horn is very highly prized in some countries in the Orient. Some people there believe, quite mistakenly, that the substance obtained from the rhinoceros horn acts as a love potion. As a result of the trade in horn, the Javan and Sumatran rhinoceros became very rare indeed. So, people began to trade in rhino horn from Indian and African rhinos, which are now also endangered.

In Africa, the white rhinoceros was the first to become rare. The white rhinoceros is large and much less wary than the black rhinoceros, and was therefore easier to hunt. It was not until the 1950s that it was realized the black rhinoceros was also threatened. Now, both species are mostly confined to nature reserves. Even so, the protected rhinoceros is still in danger from poachers anxious to profit from the demand for its horn. Most of these people are very poor, often on the brink of starvation, and so are willing to take the risk of being fined, or even imprisoned, for the sake of the money they can get for the horn.

Ox-peckers explore the hide of this black rhinoceros, hunting for ticks and other parasites.

Rhinoceros numbers

The map shows the distribution of the five living species of rhinoceroses. The table shows how many of each species still survives. Only the African black rhinoceros exists at all in any numbers outside game reserves.

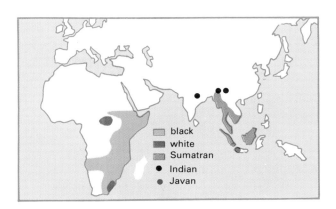

black
white
Sumatran
● Indian
● Javan

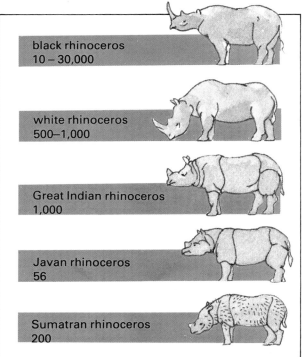

black rhinoceros
10 – 30,000

white rhinoceros
500–1,000

Great Indian rhinoceros
1,000

Javan rhinoceros
56

Sumatran rhinoceros
200

The skin trade

The luxury fur and leather trades account for the needless slaughter of many wild animals. Rare and beautiful animals, like the snow leopard from the Himalayas, are hunted for their skins, though there are now only enough left to make a few coats.

Crocodile and alligator skins are much in demand for articles such as shoes, handbags and wallets. As a result, their hides fetch a very high price, and they are hunted and killed in all parts of the world where they still exist. At first, only the larger specimens were killed, but as these became scarcer, the smaller ones met the same fate. Today, at least twelve species are threatened with extinction. However, crocodiles breed rapidly and successfully both in the wild and in captivity, and it is estimated that a five to ten year ban on hunting them would enable most of the species to recover fully. Although they are not very appealing or sympathetic animals (some of them eat people on occasions!) they are still part of the world's natural heritage, and should be allowed to survive.

It is perhaps easier to sympathize with the magnificent wild cats, which suffer because of the beauty of their skins. All the spotted cats are now very rare because of excessive hunting for the fur trade. They include leopards, jaguars, cheetahs, lynx, caracals and ocelots, as well as many others which are not so well known.

None of these animals present any threat to people. The shy leopard can live quite close to people without anyone knowing it is there at all. In fact, leopards can be helpful to humans because they kill wild

Nile crocodiles basking on a sandbank is a rare sight today, but was commonplace only 30 years ago.

Spur-wing plovers hunt their hides for parasites. The birds are tolerated because they warn the crocodiles of danger.

pigs, baboons, and other animals which are a pest to crops. Yet the spotted cats are still hunted, and the rarer they become, the more highly-prized their skins are.

In recognition of the threat to these animals, some governments have taken steps to halt the trade. Some countries where they live have banned the export of skins, while others have banned their import. Unfortunately, fur traders still manage to find ways of breaking the regulations and passing skins between countries.

The best hope for the future of these animals is to convince people that the luxury fur and skin trade is cruel and unnecessary. Many people have already realized that they can no longer wear a fur coat or crocodile shoes with a clear conscience.

The beautifully marked margay is a tree-living cat from Central and South America.

Like all spotted cats its skin is in demand by the fur trade and it could be endangered by hunters.

Animal capture

Many live animals are captured from the wild to supply zoos, pet shops and scientific research laboratories.

For most young children, a visit to the zoo is the beginning of a life-long interest in animals. But apart from the pleasure and educational interest zoos provide, they can also play an important part in conserving wildlife. The majority of zoos make sure their animals are kept healthy and happy,

Adult orangutans like this male will only continue to live in the forests of Java and Sumatra if they are protected.

and try to provide conditions in which they can breed and rear their young. These zoos will not purchase rare animals that won't breed in captivity.

Unfortunately, though, some zoos are run primarily for financial profit, with little concern for the welfare of the animals. Money is saved by cooping the animals up in small cages, and by feeding them poorly. The success of these zoos depends on having a wide range of exotic and unusual exhibits, and this often means taking rare animals from the wild, without thought for the future survival of the species.

The pet trade is also guilty of mistreating wild animals, by dealing in those which are simply not suitable as pets. Monkeys, for instance, are usually bought when they are young. But these lively, intelligent animals react badly to such a lonely, unnatural life. They grow up to become nervous, destructive and completely unmanageable.

At first, it may seem fun to keep an unusual pet. But most animals, which are used to being wild and free, can never be happy in a house. So, if you want a pet, it's better to stick to domestic animals, like dogs and cats, which enjoy human company.

In recent years there has been an increasing demand for live animals for use in scientific and medical research. Guinea pigs are specially bred for the purpose, and so there is no threat to the species, though there is constant criticism about the cruel way in which they are treated.

But animals are also taken from the wild to be used for medical research, with monkeys and apes being particularly valued since they are the species most similar to humans.

The orangutans from Sumatra and Borneo are sought after both by laboratories and zoos. Only the young are taken and the mothers are often shot so that the babies can be easily captured. Many of the young orangutans die during transportation, and many more die from human infections. Only a very small proportion of them survive into adulthood and only a few of these breed.

In the case of gorillas from Central Africa, it used to take up to forty deaths to obtain just one surviving couple for breeding in captivity. This was obviously too high a price to pay.

Nowadays, both gorillas and orangutans are regularly bred in captivity. The laws concerning the import and export of the great apes are much stricter than they used to be. They are still very rare in the wild, but this is due more to the destruction of their habitat than their capture by humans.

This mountain gorilla and its infant are still endangered by hunting and the destruction of the forests where they live. But neither mountain gorillas, nor the lowland race, suffer so severely now from being collected for zoos and scientific institutes.

17

Game hunting

All through history, rich and powerful people have indulged in the sport of hunting, and game preserves still exist in many parts of the world. These are areas of private land set aside so that game animals can breed and flourish, safely protected from poachers and other dangers. The Persian kings called their preserves "paradises"; Europeans called them parks.

Hunting is no longer just the sport of kings, but a popular sport open to many people. If hunting is regulated, the animals are not endangered. In fact, sometimes they may even benefit. This is because hunters have an interest in making sure the animals survive in plentiful numbers. The more game animals there are on a preserve, the more they can be hunted without fear of running out of stocks.

So although the animals are preserved in order to be hunted and killed, the sport can actually save some species from extinction. For example, the huge moose, which are now common in Scandinavia, thrive because they have been protected, largely for sport. When deer-hunting is forbidden during the breeding season, and hunters are given a fixed number of deer they are allowed to kill in a year, the species is not endangered.

While it seems cruel to hunt and kill these

The moose is the largest animal in Europe. Far from being rare, they are so common in Sweden that they are the major cause of road accidents outside towns. They are protected largely for hunting.

Mule deer live in the west of North America. Valued as game, their hunting is controlled. Left to themselves, their numbers would multiply because all their natural predators have been destroyed. They would then have to be killed to stop them harming farmers' crops.

beautiful, peaceful animals, it has to be remembered that the threat of violent death has always been part of their life. In nature, predatory animals hunt and kill herbivores (or plant-eating animals). Few of them ever die of old age.

Many large predatory animals, like wolves and pumas, have almost been exterminated. Because the deer have fewer natural enemies, hunting is sometimes necessary in order to keep their numbers down. The deer in America, for instance, would reach plague proportions in some places if their numbers were not controlled by hunters.

While regulated hunting is unlikely to cause too much damage to a valued species, unrestricted hunting and the hunting of rare animals can cause great harm. "Big game" hunting has been condemned all over the world because there are not enough large wild animals left. Polar bear hunting used to be a popular sport. The hunters simply flew over the ice-caps in a helicopter until they spotted a bear. The animal was an easy target to shoot, and the "sport" involved no skill or bravery on the part of the hunter. Now all the nations which surround the Arctic seas, where the polar bears live, have agreed to protect them.

Père David's deer ceased to live wild in north-east China about 3,000 years ago. But it was kept for hunting in parks there until the last century.

Now it lives only as a park or zoo animal in many places in the world. If it had not been protected for hunting, it would have become extinct long ago.

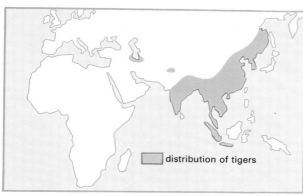

distribution of tigers

Seven races of tigers lived in Asia and the East Indies. The largest, shown here, is the very rare Manchurian tiger. The smallest, from Bali, is now extinct. No more than 5,000 of all races are probably left in the wild.

The most numerous is the Bengal tiger from the Indian subcontinent. There could be 2,000 of these, nearly all living in reserves. Without such reserves, it is hard to see how tigers can continue to live wild.

Predators

Predatory animals are meat-eaters which kill other animals for food. They mostly hunt wild animals, but sometimes they also kill livestock and game animals. For this reason they have always been hunted by humans, and singled out as our enemies. The largest predators have suffered most.

Wolves have been particularly persecuted because of an age-old belief that they attack and kill people, even though there is no evidence to support this. Today, they are very rare in the wild and only survive in remote areas. The tiger, however, does sometimes justify its reputation as a man-eater, and so cannot be allowed to live near humans. Tigers have been mercilessly hunted and can now only survive if they are protected in reserves.

Predatory animals are often killed on sight by hunters and farmers, and there are now many endangered species. In Europe, lynx, martins, polecats, otters and stoats have been so ruthlessly hunted that they are now extremely rare. Yet none of these animals are a really serious threat to livestock or game animals. Foxes and coyotes are destroyed because they kill chickens, ducks and turkeys. But farmers tend to forget that predators also do a useful job in killing countless small rodents which are extremely destructive to crops.

Predators can also help to keep game animals healthy by killing the sick and injured. In America, snapping turtles were killed because it was thought they ate the game fish. It was then discovered that where the turtles survived, the game fish grew bigger and healthier. In fact, the turtles preyed on smaller fish which competed with the game fish for food.

Many more predatory animals could survive if we changed our attitude towards them and recognized that they can be helpful as well as destructive.

Snapping turtles (above) are no longer seen as enemies by anglers. But coyotes (right) are still killed in many American states. In one state they were killed as predators of game birds. But the numbers of birds did not rise, but fell because the eggs and fledglings of the birds were being taken by rats and other small predators. The coyotes had kept these in check before. Now, more enlightened states view coyotes as friends.

Wildlife reserves

Wildlife reserves are protected areas of natural habitat set aside for the wild animals and plants which live there. Many previously threatened species have recovered since reserves were first established.

The idea started in America, in the nineteenth century, when a group of travellers came across an area of outstanding beauty, rich in animal life. Realizing how easily it could be spoiled, they persuaded the government to declare it a national park, to be left untouched by humans. So Yellowstone Park, as it became known, was the first of many nature reserves and national parks all over the world.

Since then, many huge national parks have been established in North America and Africa, where there were still large areas of uninhabited land. In Europe, where most of the land is settled, smaller reserves have been set up.

For some of the larger animals, reserves provide the only chance for survival. But even here they are not always completely safe. The rare Asiatic lions of the Gir Forest in India, have been protected there for about one hundred years. But some years ago their safety was threatened when local people began to invade the forest. Trees were felled to make space for farmland, and over-grazing by domestic cattle destroyed many areas which had supported antelopes, deer and wild pigs, on which the lions preyed. When the lions turned to cattle for food, people shot or poisoned them.

The number of lions fell drastically until action was taken by the Indian government, assisted by world conservation organiza-

tions. The local people were given alternative land, and a long stone wall was built to keep cattle out of the sanctuary.

The management of reserves is a difficult task and requires constant attention. In Africa, for instance, elephants can cause a lot of damage if their numbers are allowed to get out of control. Large herds in too small an area are very destructive to the landscape, destroying vegetation and uprooting trees. A population of 20,000 elephants in Tsavo National Park in Kenya reduced much of the area to semi-desert. Over-crowding is dangerous for the elephants and for other animals on the reserve. Starvation becomes a threat because there is not enough vegetation to go round. In this case, some elephants have to be killed in order to save the rest.

The Spanish lynx is one of the rarest mammals in Europe. Only a few hundred exist, mostly in the Coto Doñana which is now a nature reserve. It is one of the last unspoiled areas of wilderness and wetland left in Europe. It is a haven for many other plants and animals besides the Spanish lynx.

These African elephants need a great deal of space if they are not to destroy their own habitat and starve. Even in the biggest reserves in Africa, a close watch has to be kept to make sure their numbers do not exceed the food supply.

23

Captive breeding

When a species becomes so rare that extinction is almost certain, captive breeding may offer a chance of survival. This involves taking a few of the surviving animals from the wild in the hope that they will breed in captivity where they can be carefully nurtured and protected. Captive breeding is tried only as a last resort because of the risks it entails. There is the danger of death or injury during capture or the animals may fail to breed.

Despite some failures, there are successes. Both the European bison and Przewalski's horse owe their existence to captive breeding. In 1930 there were no European bison in the wild, and only thirty animals in zoos. Through a careful captive breeding program these animals increased their numbers. They now thrive in special reserves in Russia and Poland.

Przewalski's horse, the only truly wild horse in the world, is on the point of extinction in the remote deserts of Mongolia where it is found. But the species as a whole is safe because many of these horses are now bred in zoos across the world. In fact there are probably more of them in captivity than there are in the wild.

The Arabian oryx is another example of successful breeding. They were severely endangered because of over-hunting. Then, several dozen were transported to the Phoenix Zoo in Arizona, to be bred in captivity. Eventually some were returned to the Arabian deserts, where they now thrive, protected by the Harassis tribesmen.

Captive breeding is becoming an increasingly important function of zoos, although it is not an easy task. Many wild animals, such as the panda, are very reluc-

Saving the oryx

Once, it was a great feat for a Bedouin Arab to shoot an oryx. Only after days of patient tracking could it be killed. Then cars and modern guns became available. It became very easy to chase the oryx by car, and shoot it when it stopped from exhaustion.

Because of uncontrolled hunting, the Arabian oryx had become very rare by the 1960s. Three were caught to join others already captive in zoos.

tant to breed in captivity, and others simply will not breed at all.

Zoologists are learning more about breeding and rearing wild animals. A great deal of work goes into creating the right conditions for breeding, and providing surroundings which are as similar as possible to the animals' natural habitat. As techniques improve, hopefully more and more animals will be saved from extinction.

But there are other problems. Some animals, particularly predators, can become too tame to go back into the wild, because their parents cannot teach them to hunt and kill in captivity. It is also a sad possibility that some animals will never be able to return to the wild because their natural habitat has been completely destroyed. Some species may then have a future only as zoo animals.

Cheetahs tame easily and have long been used for hunting. But they had never bred in captivity. Recently, it was found that females prefer to mate with a strange male.

Now cheetahs are bred in captivity and the species should be safe. In both Africa and Asia they have become very rare in the wild where they are victims of the trade in exotic furs.

A breeding herd of oryx was started in Phoenix Zoo, Arizona, where the climate was similar to that of Arabia. The captive oryx thrived.

Other captive herds were begun. Some were returned to the Arabian desert where they are protected by the Harassis people – who, not long ago, used to hunt them.

Animal farm

People have always looked after animals which are useful to them, and for this reason most farm and domestic animals have prospered. But it is also in our own interests to preserve wildlife, because many wild animals may be valuable in future.

The kouprey, for instance, is a rare species of wild cattle discovered in Indo-China in 1936. The long and bitter wars in that part of the world seriously affected the wildlife there, and only a few kouprey have managed to survive. But they are thought to be the only cattle in the world which are immune to rinderpest, a common tropical disease which kills many farm cattle. If enough kouprey are saved, it might be possible to use them to develop a breed of cattle which is resistant to the disease.

In Africa, a rich variety of wild grazing animals used to flourish on the savannah. They did not compete with each other for food because different species eat different kinds of vegetation. But since domestic cattle have been introduced on to the savannah, there has no longer been enough grazing land for the wild species, and many of them have been driven out. If the land is over-grazed by cattle, it is eroded and becomes semi-desert. The wild animals then lose their habitat, and the land becomes useless for cattle-raising.

Here again, these animals could be extremely useful to us. Many countries in Africa are poor, and its peoples desperately in need of protein to stay healthy, or even survive at all. More meat could be provided for them if a variety of wild savannah animals could be farmed instead of cattle.

They have done this in Russia where the saiga antelopes are culled every year for

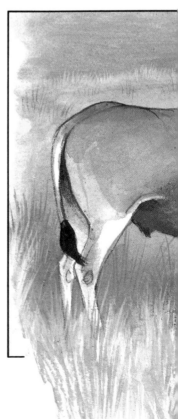

Saiga antelope were once very rare in Russia. Now they are protected as the animals best able to exploit the arid steppes there.

meat and hides. Once very rare, they are now bred and protected, and live in enormous herds on the arid steppes.

The vicuna, a South American relative of the camel, has been almost destroyed by us, despite its usefulness in providing the best quality wool in the world. It is believed that in ancient times there were more than a million vicunas. The Incas used to round them up every four years and shear them.

But more recently, vicunas were hunted and killed in such vast numbers that they became very rare. By 1968 there were only 12,000 left, and they were declared an endangered species. The South American nations joined together in banning all trading in vicuna wool, while other countries agreed to ban imports of the wool. Now that the vicunas have recovered, it is hoped that people will learn from the Incas.

Vicunas live in herds on the slopes of the Andes at heights up to 20,000 feet.

eland

Domestication

No African game animal has been successfully domesticated, although Russians have tried for a long time with the eland from Africa. Attempts are being made to domesticate the Thomson's gazelle, which could yield twice as much meat as cattle on the same grazing. Blesbok are no longer found in the wild, but are kept on many South African ranches for meat. But they are not truly domesticated.

blesbok

Thomson's gazelle

The power of humans

Humans are the most successful animals on earth. Our numbers have increased more than any other species, and our intelligence is unsurpassed. Because of these great advantages, we have conquered the world, changed our surroundings, and claimed most of the world's land for our own use.

But now we are becoming increasingly aware of the effect this has had on animal life. Throughout history we have hunted wild animals and taken their territory. We have deprived them of their breeding grounds and their natural sources of food. We have poisoned the rivers and the lands with the chemical products of our industrial society. As a result, an alarming number of wild animals are threatened, and many have already become extinct.

Most of the destruction we have caused has been carried out in ignorance of what the consequences would be. People used to think that nature was boundless and incapable of being destroyed. It is only in the last hundred years or so that it has dawned on us that this is simply not true.

But it is not too late to make up for some of the damage we have done. In recent years, efforts to stop the extermination of wild animals have been more and more

A cheetah surveys a herd of gazelles on the African savannah. If such a sight is not to become a thing of the past, then people everywhere will have to combine to save these animals, and the wilderness to which they are so well adapted.

successful, and animal lovers all over the world are joining together to take action. The human population is growing constantly, and putting more and more pressure on the wild animals that still remain. This means that the animals need constant help from us in order to survive.

If enough people help in small ways, a tremendous amount can be achieved. You can help by joining one of the many conservation societies.

Index

Illustrated by Maurice Wilson and David Cook